Sad Cats

Barbara Melons

Misty's owner passed away two years ago. She's been waiting by the window since.

When will you be home?

My tummy hurts.

Butters ate an entire can of tuna.

This isn't a sweater!

Kiki wanted a sweater for her birthday,
but her owner knitted her
a scarf instead.

He's my only friend.

It's true. Nobody likes Toothpick.

Little did Molly Know
she would be euthanized
that night.
I'll always stay
by your side.

You touched <u>another</u> cat.

Candy will never forgive her owner.

I thought I was special.

Her daddy prefers the company of humans.

Why can't I go out to play? Because the world is a dangerous place.

It's not your fault.

Max was hit by a car. His right leg had to be amputated.

I didn't eat the pie.

This pussy's a liar.
She'll eat your pies
again when you're
not looking.

Where are all my toys?

After chewing through the sofa,
this fiend won't get to have anymore fun.

Those heels will be
torn to shreds by morning.

You have all the fun!

This thug is getting neutered tonight.

No more fights, I promise.

A dog bit off one of her ears.

I'm a tough girl.

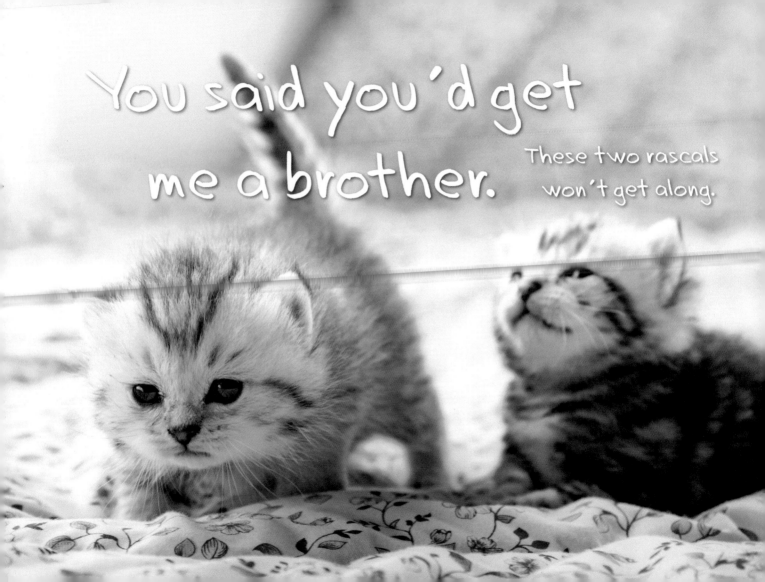

I'm sorry I'm not a dog.

His owner tried to teach him fetch, but he just couldn't get it.

Do you think I'm fat?

Muffins weighs over 100 pounds.
He has diabetes.

I bumped my head
on the coffee table.

Actually, her owner hit her.

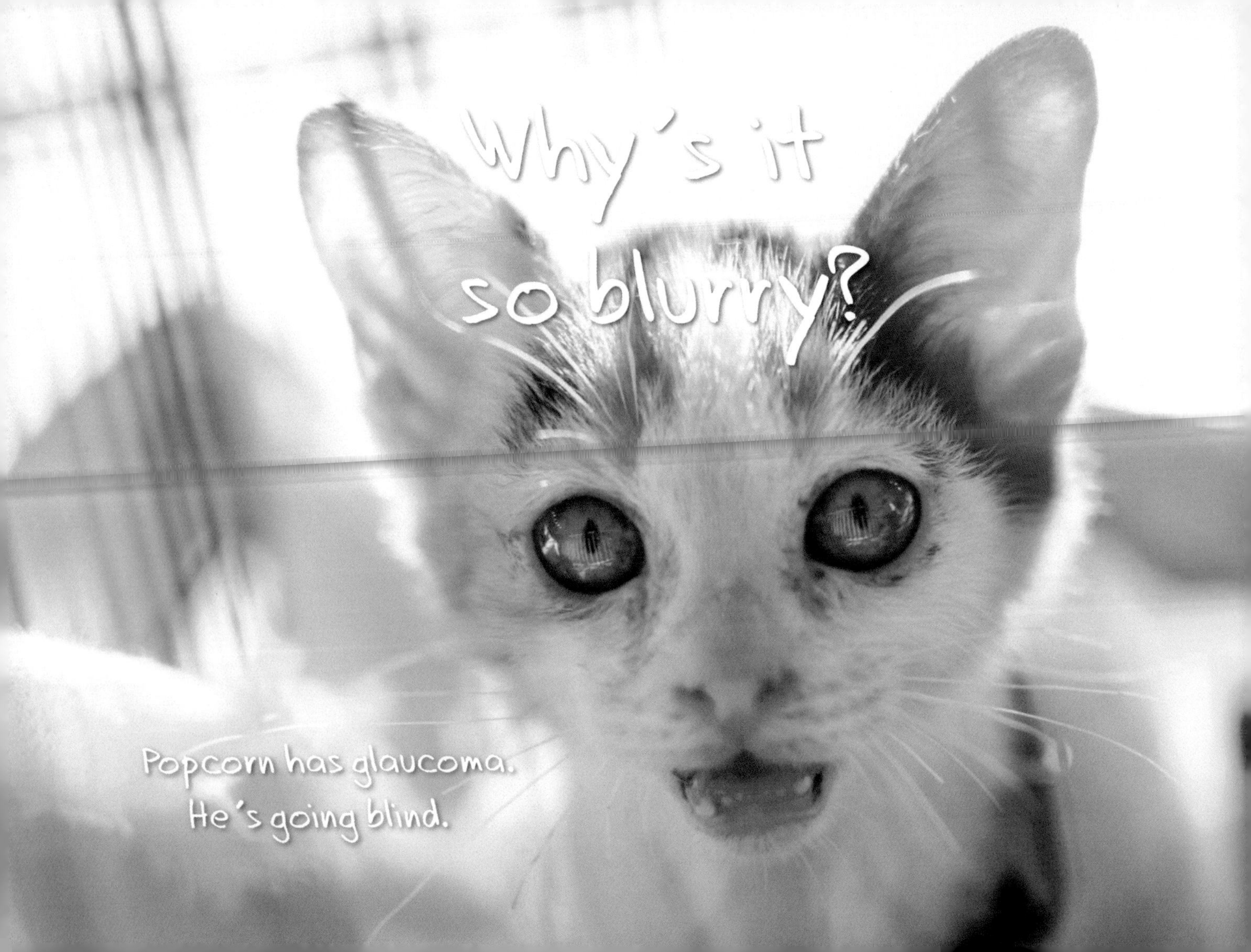
Why's it so blurry?
Popcorn has glaucoma.
He's going blind.

Too poor to support her luxurious lifestyle,
Mimi's family is forced to surrender her to an animal shelter.

Please
don't give me away!

Pepper's planning to run away from home.

I hate it when you do that.

I want to see my babies!

Coco went through a tough labor.
None of her kittens survived.

This is punishment for being a bad kitten.

It's lonely in here.

I didn't mean
to scratch you.
No more pretty nails for this young lady.

This time, she's getting spayed.

The vet again?

No, I won't kiss you!

Garlic had all his teeth extracted recently.
He's too ashamed to give anymore kisses.

Take this stupid thing off me!

She 'll have to wear the cone for another month.

Please don't yell at me.

Don't fall for it.
She's a rebel.

The birds don't sing anymore.

They do sing.
Mimi doesn't know she's become deaf.

Who's that on your lap?

Her daddy has a new girlfriend.

The next morning, he was found sprawled on the sidewalk, motionless.

Nobody wants me.

I can't find
my way home.

He'll join the 50 million stray cats
that roam the streets of America.

ISBN: 978-1973258148
Edition: 1.0

Printed in Poland
by Amazon Fulfillment
Poland Sp. z o.o., Wrocław